Raised In His Ways

Teaching Christian Values in the Early Childhood Years

Mary Annthipie Bane

ISBN: 1479238104
ISBN-13: 978-1479238101

Scripture Verses from the King James Version and the New International Version of the Holy Bible.

DEDICATION

"Raised In His Ways" is dedicated to my three sons: Tyler, Cooper and Wesley whom I love with all of my heart and I am blessed to be called their mom. To my husband and best friend Terence who has taken this journey with me.

Always I will offer my praise to my God and I am thankful to have been called to be His child, He has given me a hope and a future. Jeremiah 29:11

ACKNOWLEDGMENTS

I would like to take a moment to acknowledge all of the families I have had the privilege to come to know and love and whose children I have cared for and taught. My thanks to my brothers and sisters in Christ that I have called friends; in the churches I was blessed to attend, community organizations and in preschools, daycares and learning centers that I have been so happy to be a part of. I will forever pray for God's blessings on all of the children and families I have known. I lift them up to the Lord in the Name of the Father, and of the Son and of the Holy Spirit. Amen.

Chapter One

An Introduction

I was inspired to write Raised in His Ways after my many years as an early childhood education professional, a Christian education worker and most importantly as a mother of three sons. I am still in the process of raising my boys who are now well into their teen years, I have seen the benefits of instilling in them good Christian values that they would use as a guide in making decisions, choices and friendships. It was a priority for me that my children would be introduced to the most important relationship in their life and this is the one with the Lord and Savior Jesus Christ. For me it was my divine appointment to nurture their spiritual lives and give my children good and godly Christian roots so that as they grew and matured they would develop the fruit of their faith. I remind myself that the children belong to our heavenly Father and it is my responsibility as parent, and in our family together with my husband to raise them in His ways. As I have written in my first book "Following the Shepherd's Staff," I was not brought up in a church community. We did celebrate Christmas and Easter and believed in God. My father was a good, honest and hardworking man who instilled in his children a work ethic and a love that was firm and steady. He was a man of inner strength and he met his responsibilities to his wife, home and family diligently. For a brief time I visited a neighborhood church while I was in kindergarten but my church attendance there was short lived. My mother was diagnosed with Rheumatoid Arthritis and not physically well enough for regular church attendance. Through no fault of her own and having given her very best efforts my mother was unable to continue any religious training on my behalf. I do have fond memories of Sunday school classes, hymns and Easter Lilies. The first hymn that I can recall is "We are One in the Spirit" and it was this hymn that was played for me at the age of thirty-three when I was baptized as a born-again believer, bringing me back to my own early roots of faith. While growing up ours was not a house of outward prayer or seeking God's will, these were private for my parents. I did however learn these important life lessons in that Kindergarten Sunday School class that I have always remembered throughout my growing up years. These truths that I held dear are that Jesus longs to be my friend, that when we pray to God we can simply talk to him in the same way we would talk to our father and family and that every Sunday is like a "Little Easter." The latter comes to mind and always evokes a smile to think that on each and every Sunday morning we remember the sacrifice that Jesus made on the cross at Calvary and his glorious resurrection as He took the punishment for our sins and provided us with a way of redemption and forgiveness.

I would have occasions to go to a church

service from time to time, a christening, a wedding or an invitation from a friend would lead me on a Sunday morning to a variety of churches with varying denominations. On these visits I added to my knowledge that we are to love the Lord our God with all our heart, treat each other the way we would like to be treated and we are to honor and obey our parents, all of which I tried to do.

With this most basic of Christian instruction I navigated childhood, the teen years and early adulthood. I married and joined the Catholic Church and then at that time I made a conscious decision to ask Jesus

Christ into my heart and life, I recognized my need for a Savior in a new way and began to build on those first early steps of faith.

Looking back now as a mother of three sons ages eighteen, fifteen and thirteen, I cannot help but recall my own growing up years with the struggles, challenges, heartbreaks and joys that came along. I realize now that my few small mustard seeds of faith, carried me through it all. I cannot help but wonder how different my choices, truth and consequences would have been if I had been more fully raised in His ways. Since the birth of my first son I have directed my steps towards the education of young children and have a special love for sharing the Christian faith, morals and values with these little ones; encouraging them along the way as they too are raised in His ways.

Chapter Two

Come to Him

Jesus said, "Let the little children come to me, and do not hinder them, for the kingdom of heaven belongs to such as these." Matthew 19:14. Jesus instructed his disciples to bring the children to him and allow them to draw near to him. We are likewise to follow this instruction, for the kingdom of God belongs to the children of God. If the children of the church are not participating in Christian Education programs either in their local church or through home education they are vulnerable for growing into their teen years and young adulthood with a value system which is similar to that of the secular society. Christian parents and educators are mandated by the great commission to spread the Gospel of Christ through all the nations. This act of evangelism must begin with our youngest children for Christianity to endure throughout the coming generations.

The absence of a Christian education in the formative early childhood years, I believe, is a contributing factor leading to challenging and undesirable behaviors in children and adolescents. The neglect of teaching the basic tenets of Christianity beginning in preschool can lead a child astray from the faith, lending the child to have no interest in considering living their Christian values and having no understanding of Biblical teachings according to God's Word. Every moment spent with a child is an opportunity to guide their spiritual development, the importance of which cannot be underestimated. The training of a child who is not a Christian in the ways of biblical teachings has moral benefits that will help the child to develop, regardless of their religious affiliation.

Raising a morally sound child requires investing your time in teaching that child to live by the most basic and fundamental truth which is to live by what has become to be known as God's Golden Rule. According to Luke 6:31, "And as ye would that men should do to you, do ye also to them likewise." It is a most basic and seemingly simple truth, to do to others as you would have them do to you, yet the fabric of a moral society depends on it. We are instructed by Jesus to treat other people the way that we would like to be treated. This is a truth that the youngest preschool aged child can understand and obey. In the early childhood education classroom it is often the first biblical concept that is taught. This truth is not only taught in a Christian educational environment but also in secular preschools. It is timeless, relevant and both spiritual as well as practical.

Long before a child enters Kindergarten he or she has the parent as first teacher. A child who is in a full time daycare program may spend more time daily with the caregivers than with their own parents. It is vital that a child have a continuity of teachings and trainings. Parents with strong Christian values and beliefs must instill these values into their children. While I do believe that the removal of prayer from our schools was not in the best interests of our children, it is ultimately the parent's responsibility to begin the child's day with prayer, if they so choose. This obligation extends to finding caregivers who share and support those values for the purpose of continuity of structure, training and nurturing for the child. This is not to suggest that we are to teach "religion" to these children but values, kindness, caring, and a love for truth.

Children must make a moral connection between themselves and the people around them. I have observed in my experience that the first five years of life is the window that is open wide to this character formation training. Beyond the basic right and wrong rules of society the child must learn the answer to the question, "Why?" Why should a child respect those in authority? Why should a child honor and obey their parents? Why should they display character traits of being trustworthy, respectful and caring? It is crucial to the spiritual and character development of children to provide them with a foundation of values that is the framework in understanding God's sovereignty over their lives.

Instructing children in the way they should go is to impress upon their hearts the truth of God's Holy Word, how it applies to their lives and the manner in which they conduct themselves. We as Christians are to train up a child in the way he should go, and as promised in Proverbs 22:6 when he is old, he will not depart from it. It is true, as they grow they may stray but God promises that His word shall not return void and that these children will be brought back to Him.

The Bible tells us to “Listen and be wise and keep your heart on the right path” Proverbs 23:15-19. The teachings that we provide to our children do not only educate the mind. Christian education is designed to turn the heart to God’s truth, to wisdom and knowledge of His ways, which are greater than our own. Providing a child with a seminal instruction will give that child and all children moralities and fundamentals which will guide them throughout their lives.

Simple Biblical truths can be taught in the early childhood education years and understood by the young child. Our children must learn and treasure in their hearts these truths: Jesus loves them, they are to honor and obey their parents, they are to love the Lord with all of their hearts, souls, minds and strength, to love their neighbor, to treat others the way they want to be treated. We have a sense of the importance of God's Word in Deuteronomy 32:46-47, "Take to heart all the words I have solemnly declared to you this day, so that you may command your children to observe carefully all the words of this law." As a guidebook the scriptures teach us that truth can be found that is useful for training and educating, creating in each individual a love of that which is good and will bring life to the hearer of His Word. Formative instruction in Christian values should not be postponed beyond the early childhood years.

The pervasive, often immoral culture will take hold of our children, creating confusion in their minds and rebellion in their hearts. Waiting to instruct them places them in peril of being lost to the nontheistic teachings of the secular world. A Christian family who is not providing a foundation of biblical teachings places their children at risk of developing behaviors that parallel their unbelieving peers. Children who are taught from early childhood that God created the world and His people and instructs us on how best to live our lives are provided an opportunity for spiritual development, to taught treasure His redemptive promises and grow to model Christian values. The children who are consistently and lovingly instructed in the ways of the Lord will mature in their relationships with Jesus Christ. I am not however suggesting that we have a debate about creation vs. evolution, or any denominational discussions Being raised in His ways is a heartfelt mindset and walk with

God. Being raised in His ways is to give the children an example of a live of morals and an understanding of whom these morals stem from and honor. I believe that God is more concerned about our hearts than about our big bang debates. Our God has written in His word that He wants us to love one another. He loves the world, He gave His Son, this love must continue through His children.

The spiritual well-being of our children is at stake. The mindset of a generation of young people can be molded by the values of the social media more than it reflects the values of their Christian parents and the church, if we are not cautious. Countless studies have set out to prove that there is more than a casual connection between media violence and aggressive, rebellious behavior in some children, although there are some who reject this notion. I have found this to be true in my own sons, and if I'm honest, in myself. If sad movies can cause our emotions to become sullen, if exciting adventures can get our hearts racing then certainly the second hand experiences of violence and aggression can and do play a part in altering our mindsets. I am not suggesting a ban on such games and movies but exposure to the developing mind of a child too young will alter their thinking patterns; discernment is essential. Children are what they live, see, think, hear and experience; whether harmless or harmful. Parents as their children's first teachers are responsible for guarding what their children are exposed to. Christian parents are called to set their children's minds on the things above rather than earthly things as it is written in Colossians 3:2 "Set your affection on things above, not on things on the earth." Our children will be transformed by the world if they are not trained in their preschool years to “love what is pure, hate what is evil and to cling to what is good” Romans 12:9. I’ve been through this battle in my own home. It is my experience that it is far easier to guide without the undesirable influence in the early years.

As Christians who are obedient to the Word of God we are called to spread the goodness of the Gospel of Christ to all the nations. This mandate begins in the home and we must remember to impart this good news on to our children lest they should become morally and spiritually bankrupt. The lure of television, internet, video games and the acceptance of friends will prevail in our children if their hearts are not grounded in the teachings of Christ.

How do we develop children who are of good moral character? Every individual person has their own interpretation of what it means to be a good person. In this effort to impart values, there is one problem that persists in raising children with a good moral foundations and that is to have a common baseline to use a rule by which to guide them, their behavior and thought patterns. Children have a natural inborn desire to please, to learn and to do well. They thrive on praise, and in my experience as a preschool teacher and a parent, they desire to "do good" but have no means by which their good is to be done on their own. Children need guidance, spiritual and moral training in a consistent, kind and loving manner. People of all ages, but particularly children in the early childhood years are to be trained to seek out and desire that which is good. Children are also born with a nature that is apt to do those things which it should not do, guidance is essential for a child's moral growth.

Children are naturally self-absorbed and

impulsive. They need to be taught to see that none render evil for evil unto any man; but ever follow that which is good, both among yourselves, and to all men" 1 Thessalonians 5:15. A young child's character is developed at the very beginning of his or her life by the value system that is held by the influencing adults, adults who recognize that it is God's standard by which we characterize a thing as having "goodness". Children display moral behavior before they are able to communicate through expressive language. Infants through toddlers are able to convey whether they are bossy, cranky, are hard to please or have a disagreeable disposition. Parents, teachers and caregivers can learn to recognize these habits and be proactive, heading them off at the onset and redirecting them; easing the transition as children grow into individuals who are ready to accept moral trainings. It requires being watchful of mannerisms, of activities and the way a child is inclined to behave. It takes diligence and our goal as educators is to raise children that are an asset to their community and seek God in all that they do.

A recurrent theme in the Bible is in regards to the training of children, it has a place of biblical importance. This pertains to our own children and to the children in the community, the neighborhood and the Church. They are to be taught the ways of God and this teaching should be by example. There is unrest and a void in the hearts of young people who have been raised to disregard the presence of God in their lives. Preschool aged children who are not raised in His principles and His ways may never learn what it means to be truly obedient and responsible, may never learn to whom they are ultimately to be obedient to.

The biblical ethics which are taught

throughout Christian doctrine are described in the secular or universal world as “values” or “morals.” Christian doctrine and its teachings centered on Jesus Christ are what define Christian ethics and sets them apart from the teachings of the world. By definition it is the teachings of Christ we are to prescribe to the education of our children. People will ask, what makes these values “Christian,” other religious and humanistic teachings mirror these. In my religious tradition my moral compass is calibrated by the words of the Savior, through revelation in the scriptures and by church tradition.

Obedience to these teachings is for the honor and worship of God in three persons. People will make choices and daily decisions about how to live their lives by their own set of beliefs, their benchmark for right and wrong. Those who call themselves Christians do not base their beliefs on a set of rules or actions which they personally believe to be right or wrong but rather test them against the scriptures, against church doctrine. Christians inherit the values that have been spoken through Christ, for man shall not live by bread alone, but by every word of God, Luke 4:4. Our preschool-aged children are to be guided in this training to seek God first. Are there teachings on values from sources other than the Bible? Yes there are, there exists teachers and philosophers and experts who have their share of wisdom to impart. In my life I compare them to the words and instructions of Jesus, if they are comparable then they are worthy of my prayerful consideration.

Christian values are God given for the benefit of all mankind. The family who claims to be "Christian" but excludes church attendance and teachings from their lives may never fully grow into the blessings that

God has intended for them. Worship and church attendance may be, for various reasons, often unobserved in the home. It can happen that children families may go astray without the guidance of God's word to keep them on the straight and narrow path. Proverbs 21:16 tells us that the man that wanders out of the way of understanding shall remain in the congregation of the dead; those who are separated from God. The things of this world that are apart from God are attractive, alluring and a great temptation to our children. All too often our youth are conformed by this world rather than being transformed by the renewing of their minds, as we are reminded to be in Romans 12:2. Those individuals who are on a firm foundation of sound biblical and church tradition teachings regarding godly Christian values are promised to have the ability to stand up to any temptation in 1 Corinthians 10:13; with the way made available by our faithful God to keep yourself from it. The principles for Christian living can be found throughout the Old Testament and are also revealed in the New Testament teachings. During this time of instruction and discipleship prayer is the most important gift we can offer to the children in our care. It is through prayer by which we have a channel and a connection to the divine. Application of this instruction along with the fear of the Lord is the beginning of wisdom, Proverbs 111:10. This is not to be considered a "fear" of an angry vengeful God, but rather a healthy reverence and respect of His authority, and His praise shall endure forever. These things we can be assured of when we teach the children to come to Him.

Chapter Three

Promises and Precepts

How rewarding it is be a promise keeper. Upon the birth of my children I promised them and made a promise to myself that I would love them, always, regardless of their behavior or attitudes. I would love them. I may not always approve of their life choices, but love would be something that my sons could count on. I made a promise to myself. I promised not to judge harshly, to try to put myself in their shoes and to always remember what it was like to be a child, a teenager, restless, confused or trying to fit in. I promised my children and myself not to play the role of "mother" but to be truly myself as God has created me to be, in an authentic way, without pretense. I promised to use my God given gifts and talents to benefit and edify my family first before I would ever offer myself to others. I promised to provide mothering, training, facilitating and protecting until such a time that my sons transitioned from childhood to adulthood. I promised them that my assignment in their life would not be one of control, for only God is in control of our children and of our own selves for that matter. I will be a confidant, encourager, uplifter, mentor, comforter and friend. These are the things that I promise.

As I view my children, who are now teenagers and dealing with the anxieties of growing up in these morally trying times, I remind myself that I was once a child like them, also I am still God's child. If a fit of anger overtakes them, an unthankful attitude or spirit of rebellion, I remind myself that if I am honest, I am like that from time to time in the eyes of God. I am prone to having occasions of doubting, worrying or complaining, attributes that I am not proud of but have learned to tame over time, although not fully, lest I should boast. My growing pains continue just as those of my children do. While in the heat of any moment with my children I stop and take time to consider the ways of God, how He deals with me and in turn I try to respond to my sons in a like manner. It may be with mercy, forgiveness, understanding, or it may be with firm but loving discipline and a necessary imposed consequence.

Our God reigns and He is so good. He knows the plans He has for our lives and I remind my sons that He knew them before they were born, before the beginning of time. God had each one of them in mind by very design and desire to create and know them. We are promised this in Ephesians 1:4 “According as he hath chosen us in Him, before the foundation of the world, that we should be holy and without blame before Him in love.” God has promised to set us apart that we may be Holy, through Jesus Christ. He knew us before the creation of the world, this is what He has promised us is true. Jeremiah 1:5 tells us “Before I formed you in the womb I knew you, before you were born I set you apart, I appointed you a prophet to the nations." God again promises the knowledge, creation and care of my sons and of all children as His own. This promise is not an empty one.

For those who embrace the truth in God's words there is a joy to be found. To know you were planned by a power that is higher than your earthly parents provides a framework for seeking His will, His salvation and His Son. I have found that the teachings of a parent are more readily accepted by the child when it is known that they are based on God's truth for them and not on rules that are arbitrarily invented and imposed by mom and dad. When you live a life that is based on promises kept it will go well with you. When you are raised with this knowledge from the early childhood years it is apt to become a part of the child's nature, their very being.

Children of a very young age can understand the importance of keeping a promise. How often do you hear them ask if a friend will "promise" to be or do something special for them. Preschool aged children will "promise" to behave or play nicely with their siblings and friends. In my teaching the Ten Commandments to my children I have also taught them that they are Ten Promises that we can make.

Dear God, As you have commanded:
I promise to have no gods before you Heavenly Father

I promise I will not make any idols to worship

I promise not to misuse your name, the name of the Lord my God

I promise to remember the Sabbath day and keep it holy

I promise to honor my father and my mother

I promise that I shall not murder

I promise that I shall not commit adultery

I promise that I shall not steal

I promise that I shall not lie

I promise that I shall not covet

God's precepts are easier to understand when spoken in the language of a child. Children understand promises and the consequences when a promise is broken. Promising God to keep His commandments gives them the opportunity to choose that which is right at an early age, which will become their habit as they grow older as this desire to be a promise keeper is nurtured. The preschool years are the time to teach our children to love keeping their promises.

There is a commandment that comes with a promise of God. What glorious good news that is, to be told that when we are obedient to God and His Word, He promises something wonderful for us, it will go well with us. God's promises and His commandments are not empty. They are not void or irrelevant; they are created for our good. To be commanded to honor your father and your mother we are told it is the first commandment with a promise that when we keep this commandment it will go well with us. We will be blessed; we will walk in God's favor when we honor our father and mother. You cannot honor a heavenly Father whom we are unable to see if we are not capable of honoring our earthly father and mother.

No child will ever honor and obey their parents without fail, to expect them to would be setting the up for a fall. There is a predictable and typical amount of childhood and teenaged rebellion, back talk, pushing the boundaries and pushing parent's buttons. This is normal and to be expected, it is how they learn what is acceptable, tolerable and right. These commandments, these promises in God's Word do not guarantee perfect children perfect parents or perfect people. With promises come assurance that He will never leave us nor forsake us, no matter how hard life may become. He is our help, our strength and our comfort. These are the promises and values that I hope and pray to instill.

Chapter Four

All Things Have Become New

If any man has put his faith in Christ he is a new creation, all things have become new. That which is born of the flesh is flesh and that which is born of Spirit is of the Spirit. We are born as human creations, this is our first birth. Upon receiving the teachings of the Gospel we receive Christ as our Savior and receive our second birth, our spirits are born into a life with Jesus Christ, we are born again. The old nature of human birth becomes one in the Spirit of God and a spiritual life has begun. For the teenager or young adult this good news may be more challenging to understand or accept than for the child who is raised with this guidance of the spiritual life being their second birth. Children especially love birthdays and it is an illustration that is readily understood by the young child. A child is born and has a day of birth into the human existence. As their bodies are nurtured and grow so it is with their spiritual life until that point in time that they have their “second birth” which ushers in their life in Christ. In our family this is the time that their faith is being confirmed and a training process takes place.

In the Bible in the Old Testament and in the New we are given examples of how to train up a child. Often called a child's "religious" training, there is a method of teaching children about God. We can adapt these old ways and incorporate them into our families, making them relevant and new.

The first instances of training children in the ways of the Lord appear throughout the Old Testament and are carried through the Apostolic times and teachings of Jesus. Our earliest command to worship God is found in Exodus 34:14 "For thou shalt worship no other god; for the Lord whose name is jealous, is a jealous God," which simply put means He wants us for His own. On Mother's and Father's Day each year do we want our children visiting with the parents of their friends or do we want them for our own? So it is with God, He is and wants to be our heavenly Father. The proper worship of God must include the teaching of His Word, for worship cannot be wholly fulfilled without the knowledge and appreciative understanding of God. This command in Exodus includes children who must learn these precepts from their parents. There does not appear to be a question of age in regards to religious training. Psalm 148:12-13 states that "Both young men, and maidens; old men, and children: let them praise the name of the Lord for his name alone is excellent; his glory is above the earth and heaven." Adults and youth alike are to praise the name of the Lord. It is a parent's duty, if they desire their children to know God, to teach their children as it is written in Deuteronomy 11:19, "speaking while they are sitting at home, walking together by day and by night."

In the times of the Old Testament parents were the primary educators of their children, a responsibility that was seriously undertaken as a God given mandate. There is an abundance of references to teaching in the scriptures. The Old Testament stressed the importance of the spiritual training of children but does not indicate a system or school of formal Mosaic education. The children were to be brought to the house of God by their parents who were to train them to keep and observe the law. Proverbs 28:7 states for in this way a son is to become wise. This training would be vital if the children were not to grow up and worship false idols.

The home provided the training ground for education in the Old Testament. The Hebrew people had a purpose of learning and teaching obedience to the law God had given to them in the Torah. Life skills were a practical aspect of their teachings. This would certainly have begun in the early years as all of life was immersed in religious meaning and woven throughout their daily activities. Stories, conversations and modeling religious observations were the methods used to teach.

In the early years a girl would learn from her mother. She would begin her training in heritage and household skills. The Jewish people had available to them religious education that was administered by priests and prophets as detailed in Leviticus 10:11, to teach the children of Israel all the statutes which the Lord hath spoken unto them by the hand of Moses. 2 Chronicles 17:9 is equally instructive regarding the teaching of the Law of God that they taught in Judah, and had the book of the law of the Lord with them, and went about throughout all the cities of Judah, and taught the people. The Hebrew people were taught the obedience and ordinances of the Law.

Samuel was brought to the temple by his mother Hannah in 1 Samuel 1:25-28, where she dedicated the life of this young child for whom she had prayed to the Lord. Under the guidance of Eli, Samuel was training in religious and moral instructions. From this point forward instructing boys from the age of five in formal schooling through synagogues with scholarly scribes studying the Law, reading, writing and the teaching of a trade commenced. This was early childhood education in the Old Testament tradition where character training would have been prevalent in all of the religious activities.

In the early days of the apostolic church the earliest Christians were still considered to be and referred to themselves as still being Jewish. They worshipped and lived as Jews; they would have continued to follow the holy teachings, holy days and religious rituals. These early Christians would have maintained the commandment of training up their children as commanded in Deuteronomy 4:9. The apostles led the Jerusalem church but did not institute early childhood education programs as we would understand and expect a church to have today. The role of the apostles as church educators was to train and educate the new converts, particularly in the area of grace (Reed & Prevost, 1993, p. 69-70).

In First Timothy we see that the elders teach the Word and doctrine. Parents who were themselves brought up in the Jewish tradition would be beholden to bring their children to the house of God for teachings and would continue their lessons of the faith at home. Timothy was raised up as a spiritual leader and his instruction in spiritual matters was attended to by his mother and grandmother. Religious instruction of children in the Jewish household and early Christian church was not to be neglected or delayed. Parental teachings imparting wisdom and instruction as detailed in Proverbs 1:8-9 would have been adhered to in the early church.

The new converts would realize that their faith and Christianity would not survive a generation if not imparted to their youngest children, and so it is in our modern times with our own families.

The law of God that directed parents to

train their children would be honored by the early Christian parents. As the gospel is spread throughout the early church, entire household became believers and were baptized in Acts 18:8. The children of the early church would have believing parents to guide and instruct them in the teachings of Christ, not within youth groups and activities, but with the Word of God and testimony of Jesus Christ the risen Savior and his Gospel shared through the apostles. This would be early childhood education in the apostolic church. The education of young children in matters of faith is a heritage that continues today according to each domination and it's tradition.

To historically reference Christian education one would literally translate it as: education that is designed for followers of Christ. Beginning with the work of the early church this education was to include instructing the individual who has not yet been converted, through the conversion and also encompasses learning through the post conversion experience. The preschool Christian education is designed to move the young child through his education while incorporating discipleship as the child matures in his or her faith. This is a process that is to continue over a lifetime and is best begun in early childhood. The ways of the Bible and church tradition are relevant to the spiritual training of our children today. How fortunate we are to have a guidebook to lead us in His ways for the benefit of our children that it may go well with them. Please note while I do have what would be called "religion" in my life I do not write about religion or specific denomination, but about a relationship that will guide us in raising our children.

Chapter Five

Why

Education in colonial America was primarily centered in the home and church, with the Bible being the focal point of all education. Schools were started to provide a Christian education to those who were not able to receive such training at home. I believe that to have an education and subsequent knowledge which is separated from God and His teachings is to have a misunderstanding of the truth; which is that wisdom and instruction and the benefit of such instruction comes from God himself.

Christian educators must boldly confess and understand that education from a Christian perspective holds the key to a life of knowledge of their faith and purposeful benefit, for themselves and for everyone they encounter. Today's church is a teaching institution and has planned and organized their teachings into formal educational ministries and youth programs. Today in the twenty-first century the church plays a major role and function in Christian education; alongside ministry and worship. The modern church began forming Sunday school classes in order to instill Christian values and morals to our children. In the early twentieth century Sunday church services were not to be missed and this spiritual and moral training was absolutely considered to be vital to the life of a young believer. Devoted instructors in the basic fundamental principles and beliefs of Christianity passed the faith from one generation to the next. Catechism classes are counted among the faithful instruction for many families and children.

A shift in the primary responsible party for this education began as families found it necessary to become two income households and the training of children's religious studies were delegated to church staff. What was once in the days of the Old Testament and apostolic church a daily teaching amongst families and young children now runs the risk of being designated for church classes only.

Statistics show that if a child is not raised with an immersion in the Christian faith in their daily lives that by the time the child reaches his or her teen years have fallen away from the faith completely. In a survey conducted by the Barna Group, a leading research organization whose focus is on the relationship of faith and culture, found that "less than one percent of the young adult population in the United States has a biblical worldview" (Houdmann, n.d.). Their research also found that less than one-half of one percent of Christians between the ages of 18 and 23 has a biblical worldview.

"Additionally, two studies conducted by both the Barna Group and USA Today, found that nearly seventy-five percent of Christian youth leave the church after high school. One of the key reasons they do so is intellectual skepticism" (Houdmann, n.d.). This is a result of our youth not being taught the Bible in their homes or in church and for seeing their faith as irrelevant. Statistics show that our kids today spend an average of thirty hours per week in public schools where they are being taught ideas that are diametrically opposed to biblical truths. Then they come home to another thirty hours per week in front of a television, being bombarded by lewd commercials and raunchy sitcoms, or "connecting" with friends on the social networking sites staying online for hours, chatting with one another, or playing games. There is a good and proper time for these activities but many people may find that their child spends a disproportionate amount of time in them. Whereas the time spent weekly in the church or church classroom is forty-five minutes. I would come then as no surprise that our young people leave the home as young adults without a Christian worldview or giving any thought to their value system. This time in the life of a young person needs to be balanced with spiritual nurturing and instruction; not only are they not being well-grounded in the faith, but they're also not being taught to intelligently examine the views of the skeptics who will inevitably challenge their faith. Most of these students are not prepared to enter the college classroom where the possibility exists that they will encounter people, fellow students and professors alike who view Christians with hostility and take every opportunity to belittle them and their faith.

Time Magazine in its April 2, 2007 edition featured a cover article which was titled "Why We Should Teach the Bible in the Public School." Featured in this article is a Texas Public High School that began offering a bible literacy class. Seated in this class were students who were raised in the Christian tradition alongside students who were not. While the goal of this class was to teach the bible as an object of study and not as God's Word, the school system recognized the value of this teaching to their students. The lack of teaching biblical principles beginning in the preschool years has become evident and has left a void that this high school was trying to fill. According to "Religious Literacy" polls show that nearly two-thirds of Americans believe that the bible holds the answers to all or most of life's basic questions." However in contrast a Gallop poll has indicated that the United States of America is a nation of biblical illiterates. “Only half of American adults know the title of even one gospel, most cannot name the bible’s first book” (Van Biema, 2007). This trend extends beyond unbelieving Americans as this same statistic shows that among evangelical teens only forty-four percent could identify a verse coming from the Sermon on the Mount.

The Bible is the most influential book ever written. It contains the powerful testimony of the life, death and resurrection of Jesus Christ, who came that we may have life. It is the Bible that is used in a court of law and in swearing in of our elected officials for the simple reason that it is and contains God's absolute truth. Truths that are for all people as promised in John 3:16; For God so loved the world that he gave his only begotten Son that whoever shall believe in Him shall have eternal life. This truth is meant for and understandable by the believer in the early childhood years.

For the benefit of their moral development Christian parents have access to the living words of Jesus and can raise their children to walk in the ways of the Spirit and according to the teachings of the Ten Commandments found in Exodus 7:1-17.

Children can and desire to have love, joy, peace, patience, kindness, goodness, gentleness, self-control, faithfulness which are the Fruit of the Spirit found in Galatians 5:22-23. These spiritual attributes develop in children much in the same manner that children are to progress from simple to more complex reasoning and understanding of the concepts of right and wrong.

Jean Piaget is an early childhood education theorist. Piaget studied the reactions of preschool children to the rules of playing games, the benefits of having rules and their responses to short stories that focused on moral issues. A two stage theory of moral development emerged. The first stage is a forming sense of obligation and obedience. This awareness takes place between the preschool child and at least two other persons. This sense of obligation begins to emerge at the age of four and can continue to develop through age eight. During this developmental stage the individual in the early childhood years strives to play and live within the rules. A child at age four is beginning to accept that rules and the word of adults are to be received as truths which are offered to them and they trust in these truths and are obedient to them.

During the second stage identified by Piaget, later at around age eight children are developing an awareness of fairness and begin to change their mindset of absolute adult authority and more fully develop friendships, respectfulness and a spirit of cooperation. Children of this age are concerned with consequences and once they pass through the early childhood years they will no longer react to simply wanting to please adults and are becoming able to use reasoning and are more democratic in their thinking (Essa, 2007, p. 415).

While Piaget's studies have found that a preschool child is not capable of moral judgment they do respond to stories about moral dilemmas and are capable of the idea of helping others in need. They are fully capable of understanding the concept of treating other people the way they would like to be treated themselves, which is a biblical concept. Consequences are a teaching tool which is an attribute that is developing at this stage and is understandable to the preschool aged child. It is at this age when a preschooler will be most receptive to embracing the command to honor and obey their parents with the addition of the promise that it will go well with them.

The moral development of preschoolers is a long-term process that has many contributing factors. It has been my experience that preschool aged children observe the behaviors of others, how they are treated and consequently will develop determinations of their own sense of right and wrong. Children learn according to what they live. It is imperative to their moral and spiritual development for a child to have parents and caring adults who are modeling examples of living a Christian life.

As parents we care for our infants and in return they develop a sense of security and a trust that is the result of caring, loving attention which offers the child a reciprocal respect. As our infants move into toddlerhood and the early childhood education years they can trust and believe their parents, adult caretakers and teachers who tell them about a loving God who is the Creator of the universe and who also cares about them. The developmental window of opportunity for a child to form a good and godly moral fiber is during the early childhood years and it is vital that this formation be attended to and nurtured as the child matures and faces the often turbulent teen years.

Some say that our national heritage is rooted in Christian-Judeo principles and has experienced growth and prosperity as a society as a result for over two hundred years while we have based our ideals from the words of wisdom that are found in scripture. In recent decades however there has been a falling away from morality. Our teenagers are in peril of growing up in a culture driven society and being molded by the values that society dictates. There are many Americans who call themselves “Christian” yet of there are generations of children that do not regularly attend church and are bible-believing Christians. I write about church attendance in my book “Following the Shepherd’s Staff.” Church is the body of believers and is personal. My family tradition is Roman Catholic although we have spent several years attending protestant denominations. In each we have found that the heart of the matter is to become as one who desires to be God honoring and relationship building with our Savior Jesus Christ. Many families opt for home church as they do home school and as long as God is given the glory and is worshipped that is church for them. However, there are children and teenagers who are growing up in a culture that mocks our national motto "In God We Trust," are being educated in schools that have had prayer removed and where the image of Jesus and His cross have been removed from our government and city properties. These words and images can be removed from the outward displays in our society but not from our hearts. If the trend to marginalize Christianity continues, the values of our children are at risk. This is the situation for our children; they need to be raised with proper moral guidelines, in the denomination and tradition that the family sees fit, for my family it is Roman Catholicism. This training is for the benefit of their conduct, thought patterns, habits and actions. If they are not spiritually nurtured in the Christian tradition from the early childhood years they are at risk of falling into the snares of rebellion accompanied by spiritual and life threatening events as they mature.

Teens face a myriad of temptations. Premarital sex, drug and alcohol use, crime and violence are not known only to the unbelieving teen. The Christian youth is under pressure to learn the balancing act of living their faith while living in this world though they are to not to be transformed by this world. Prayer is the first weapon in the battle for the spiritual lives and well-being of our children. To pray for them and to teach them how to seek God's guidance and protection will give the teen strength, comfort and assurance as they navigate the worldly influences of our society. It is difficult to overcome a temptation for a person of any age. These are the reasons why a youth will need the faith and the understanding that God is with them while they make decisions that may be contrary to those being made by their peers.

Chapter Six

How

I love them, from my own blessings my three sons to those in my class and in my care. I love them and I believe that they belong to the Lord, they are gifts from Him and I hope that in some small way they may experience Him through me, not in preaching and teaching, but in responding in love, one to another. I do not teach bible lessons to the preschoolers in my class and yet I respond to them in a manner that is Christ-like and that has made all of the difference. That is church, that is purpose, that is life itself and all that is worthwhile. If Christians can learn to show the abundant love of Jesus to one another, I believe that there would be more Christians and we would all be better for it into eternity. When children know that they are loved, then they are ready and able to learn. The trust that is placed in me by the parents of my students is not something that I take for granted and not something that I take lightly; it is a privilege and my joy.

The children are beautiful, marvelous, miraculous and wonderful. They are also temperamental, demanding, disobedient and unkind, on occasion. Up to this point I have focused on the "why", why should we teach and guide our children to be raised in His ways and "why" should we care or bother. In this section I will address the "how", to the best of my ability, drawing on my experience. I am in no way an expert in the field but have traveled the road of child training and have picked and fought my battles accordingly. What remains is what I have learned, what has worked for me within God's framework and what I hope to share with you.

In my classroom I have found that the use of time-outs is not effective. In my years of early childhood education experience I have observed that the child will sit for the allotted time, typically one minute per age and then was still inclined to return to the challenging behavior. In my class however time-out is not an appropriate practice and is not sanctioned as an effective behavior management tool. Before a challenging behavior arrives it generally helps if the child knows what will happen next, whether it is a transition or a consequence. Redirecting the behavior or "taking a break" in library, at the easel or with some independent manipulative usually diffuses an undesirable behavior.

Asking a child if they understand why their behavior was inappropriate and having them tell back in their own words what had happened helps to both know if they understand what the mistaken behavior was and also give an opportunity to ask if they can think of a better choice that they can make. Asking the children a question is a tool to guide the child towards independently making good choices. In my classroom we have a "feelings cube" with images of a child's face of varying emotions. The children are directed to either show how they are feeling or how their actions may have made their classmate feel. I also have an "if/then" chart, featuring illustrations of inappropriate behaviors; hitting, running, pushing, throwing toys, etc., alongside an image of consequences. Rather than time-out I have implemented a loss of privilege which may be loss of choosing an activity, loss of a class helper job or loss of an item from home.

These techniques work well in my four and five year old class. A "class meeting" on the circle time rug is helpful to open a dialogue with the class to discuss any behavior issues and brainstorm how situations could have been handled differently. The consequence poster in my room was made after we had a class large group discussion about consequences and that when we do something, something else happens. I asked them things like what would happen if we run in class, throw a toy, etc. and they would give me their answers; fall down, get a boo-boo. We charted the results and I put images next to them so they can match the words to the meaning. I don't usually have to impose a loss of a privilege as a consequence but three warnings are given for my children who repeat the mistaken behavior.

I have charted a list of classroom rules that we have all come up with at the beginning of the school year in September. It lists about six things to remember: hands are for helping not hurting, use walking feet, indoor voices, carry our class materials, put things away when we are done with them, use kind words, to raise your hand rather than shouting out. I have a few children who love to be my class reporters. I gently remind them that to tattle is to try to get someone into trouble and to report is to keep someone from trouble and to help them. They do love a good report. If it's a true tattle tale instance I say to my class, "worry about?" and they answer "yourself!" and I thank them for their report and remind them we all sometimes do things that we shouldn't and with that they usually give me an "ok" and go back to their activity. This is much in line with the scriptural principal of the speck in your friend's eye and the plank in your own; Matthew 7:3-5. The tattle tale occurrences are one way that I am able to teach the children the biblical concept of not being judgmental but to be discerning and to examine their own conscience for the near occasion of “naughty.”

Every year I incorporate character training into my curriculum enhancements. Teaching the lessons of trustworthiness, respect, responsibility, fairness, citizenship and caring. The kids in my class often remind each other if there is an undesirable behavior that they are not treating each other the way they would like to be treated. I implement many kindness and manners activities with them. They say "may I please be excused" and answer me by saying "yes, ma'am." The parents are always pleasantly surprised when they start speaking like this at home.

This is the age to learn to care for other people, the charts help but it's the interactions and the redirection that guides them. It does take more effort than putting the children in a time-out, but the results are learning that lasts and moral development without opening a bible. If the scriptures and church traditions are who I am, then it will be known by my actions, behavior and demeanor alone. The children are learning to treat other people they way that they want to be treated by my modeling this behavior to them.

Chapter Seven

Go Forth

The devil prowls like a lion looking for those whom he can devour, 1 Peter 5:8. Mature Christian adults are the first line of defense against the snares that Satan has set out to trap and entangle our children. We are the parents, the teachers, the caregivers and we are responsible for the guarding of the bodily and spiritual well-being of our children. God has seen fit to place these children in our care and this is our directive.

As parents we provide for our children in numerous ways before they are even born. We give them good prenatal care; we childproof our homes for their safety and offer everything necessary for their physical care and well-being. Our children are well clothed, well feed and are watched over. It is my fervent belief that parenthood is a high calling of God. Our children need our sacrificial love, they need our time and our prayers and they need our guidance.

A good parent would never withhold food, shelter, clothing or medical cares until the children are teenagers. Equally important is the moral development and spiritual nurturing of His little ones. It begins at birth and for myself personally I began praying for my children before they were born.

We are born with a desire to know God. Deep down in every heart that has ever beat is an ember that glows and tells us that there is a God and we are desperate to seek Him. Just as an infant physically reaches out for his mother, our souls seek out and reach for the Lord. Jesus commanded to hinder not the little children to come to me, for the Kingdom of God belongs to such as these. The little one in the womb can be told that they are loved and that Jesus loves them. An infant can hear the worlds of their parents about how great their God is, they can hear what a friend we have in Jesus, and can be held while joining in family devotions and prayer times. It is never too early to tell a child that God has made everything in this world and that indeed every hair on their head has been numbered, Luke 12:7.

The preschooler who is entering the discovery phase of his development will need no introduction to Jesus and to God's Word if he or she has heard this good news from infancy. For the toddler and the preschooler who has not been prayed with, who have not had praise songs and hymns sung to them or told of God's redeeming love, the time is right for an introduction. These young children are at the perfect time to learn of the most wonderful friendship and relationship of their lives. These children are ready to meet Jesus.

Look at a preschool aged child and picture a future of rebellion, promiscuity, substance abuse and immorality. Heartbreaking isn't it? Picture if you can the teenager who does not know God, he or she has a void in their being that they are desperately trying to fill in all of the wrong ways. The time to act to protect them and to teach them is during the early childhood years, before they reach this critical point. We would stop a preschooler from touching a hot stove and getting burned, we must guide them to stay within safe boundaries. Our children need to be taught to listen to their parent's instruction, hearing the instruction of their fathers and forsaking not the law of their mothers, Proverbs 1:8. Jesus has given us his example of shepherding and we are to tend to the spiritual education of the preschool aged child. Established Christian adults need to teach the young people to love what is pure, hate what is evil and to cling to that which is good, Romans 12:9. Our children must be guarded against opportunities for the world to teach them to love what is evil as it is written in Proverbs 24:1.

Our relationship driven teenagers will search for a place where they feel cared for and approved of. They have a great need at this age to have stability, to be grounded in love and to have a faith in the God of creation, the God of our forefathers and in His Son. They need nurturing and protective guarding against influences that may potentially cause them to fall away from the faith and into harm's way. Our teenagers need to know that God has a plan to give them a hope and a future, Jeremiah 29:11. So many teenagers experience intense loneliness and fear not fitting in with their peers. How much better for them to know from the preschool years that God will never leave them nor forsake them, as promised in Hebrews 13:5 and each of our youth is fearfully and wonderfully made, marvelous, just as they are, Psalm 139:14.

Church leaders, youth pastors and

organizations have reached out to our youth all across America. While there is good discipleship and mentoring taking place for the teen who was not brought up in a life of faith in Christ it is a bandage on a gaping spiritual wound. Parenting is critical to maintain the hearts and minds of our teens and it begins in the early childhood years. A day arrives when you wake up to find a hurting, rebellious teenager in your midst. The seeds of discontent are not sown overnight however. They are developed over time. The question is, is it better to struggle as we put in the effort to set our children back upon the good and proper path the should be on, or would it be best to set them on that path from the very beginning of their life. It is much more difficult to turn the hardening heart of a teenager than it is to instill the Christian values in our children at a young age.

Our teenagers need to be taught how to make good decisions based on God's holy teachings. As parents we have the opportunity to offer choices to our teens when they face decision making. We have the responsibility to offer choices that are within and without biblical guidelines as a guide and instruct them regarding the consequences of those decisions. This role that we play in parenting and educating will help to set a course for making right choices according to God's standards. When this decision making skill is developed in our preschoolers it will be second nature when they mature into teens.

While raising my three children I have experienced family bible readings, morning devotions and studying the bible as a school subject. During their growing up, formative years our sons were involved in children's church and Sunday school programs as well as youth groups within our local and neighboring churches. As a parent I am blessed to say that our time invested in our children has resulted thus far in a close knit family life, producing three sons who have all made a decision to receive Christ as Savior and to be confirmed in their faith. All three are growing up to treasure God's Word and their church attendance. Our journey in raising them to become men is far from over but the path is being lit by His Word.

Building a spiritual foundation in our family in no way is meant to delude ourselves into thinking that our children will not be without their faults, challenges, mistakes and share of struggles. Quite the opposite is true, when crisis situations have taken place we as parents have been able to approach and reason with our children beyond their egocentric natures. It is by gently but firmly and lovingly, consistently bringing each back to God's Word that we are able to break down any wall that has been built up of a rebellious attitude, thought or hard heartedness. It is by reminding them of who they are as Christian young men that we are able to restore them to a place of peace with God. We stumble, we fall, and we pray and seek forgiveness and more forward. It isn't perfect, easy or without its heartaches, but with God all things are possible.

After homeschooling my children the need to put them into the public school system became apparent for a variety of financial and health issues that were beyond our control. This decision seemed to be our only choice but I struggled to accept this determination even after prayerful discernment. This was a time when I felt as though I were in a spiritual wrestling match; still the decision to enroll our sons was made. The control lay as it always had and that was with God and it is in His hands that we have committed our lives and future plans. It took great faith and much prayer for me to place them in the care and teachings of others. I kept a careful watch over the new friendships that were emerging, their activities and behaviors. I was fully relying on God that their early years of biblical training would serve them well. My own children were quick to remind me that God would not leave them nor forsake them and surely He will be with them in school.

Amidst all of the secular teachings I found that my sons were able to determine for themselves those things that were good and did their best to avoid the things that were not. It was with joy, relief and thanksgiving that spiritually sound relationships had begun forming. I have given all of the thanks and praise to God that the Christian teachings for my own preschool aged children were the teachings that my children have relied on and turned to for direction on their own as they have grown.

As a Christian educator I have witnessed many wonderful young people come to know the Lord after their early childhood years and well past the beginning stages of moral development. These young people had already formed their ideas and our tolerant, permissive culture and their place in it. It is unfortunate that most had experienced the natural consequences of choices that were made which were not consistent with scriptural guidelines. All of these wayward teens would have benefited from making choices based on a moral compass and not because they couldn't seem to see any other way. The good news is that Jesus loves them, and it is never too late to turn our hearts toward God.

In my home state there is an anti-bullying

law in effect which is intended to monitor the behavior of school aged children during the school hours and also off school premises. The law, known as the Anti-Bullying Bill of Rights, is considered the toughest legislation against bullying in the nation. The law demands that every public school in the state be required to adopt the comprehensive anti-bullying policies. There are eighteen pages of "required components", an increase staff training and compliance to tight deadlines for reporting episodes. Each school must designate an anti-bullying specialist to investigate complaints; each district must, in turn, have an anti-bullying coordinator; and the State Education Department will evaluate every effort, posting grades on its Web site. Superintendents said that educators who failed to comply could lose their licenses. "I think this has gone well overboard," Richard G. Bozza, executive director of the New Jersey Association of School Administrators, said. "Now we have to police the community 24 hours a day. Where are the people and the resources to do this? "In most cases, schools are engaging guidance counselors and social workers as the new anti-bulling specialists. This raises the question of whether they have the time or experience to look into every complaint of harassment or intimidation and write the detailed reports required. Some administrators are also worried that making schools legally responsible for bullying on a wider scale will lead to more complaints and open the door to lawsuits from students and from parents who are dissatisfied with the decided outcomes (Hu, 2011). It is so very important that those who are being bullied receive the protection they need and deserve and so very sad that this need even exists at all. If only we could all treat each other as Christ has instructed us, not with malice or cruel intent but with love, acceptance and mercy.

It is my opinion that had they not taken God out of our schools we may not be seeing this widespread bully phenomenon and subsequent efforts to control it. I believe that the time of the educators and administrators would be much better spent serving the students in a manner that taught the Fruit of the Spirit. If the students will be trained in love, joy, peace, patience, kindness, gentleness and self-control perhaps the need for bully specialists and their services would no longer be required, at the very least be minimized.

Our children attend mandatory bullying assemblies and they have also experienced bullying and have witnessed bullying first hand. Our response as a family has been to discuss the situation with our children, seek God's wisdom on how to appropriately respond in a Christ-like manner to the school and the other children involved. Our belief of instilling a firm foundation has enabled us to use these "bullying" events as opportunities to grow spiritually and to mature emotionally. In spite of the school system's best efforts to keep the peace they are experiencing children who are looking for a reason to become angry and offended.

We have been able to look at these situations through the lens "What Would Jesus Do?" and what did Jesus teach? It takes a time of prayer and reflection when feelings of hurt or injustice overtake us. We need to take these thoughts captive to Christ and rely on his teachings. Times of unfairness are opportunities to build their character as we accept things we cannot change and work through options and choices that could be made if they should find themselves in difficult situations in the future. Our goal is to exercise the self-control so that they may not act out impulsively. It is unfortunate that this takes training which results from struggles. These are the times that we are able to discuss the precept "turn the other cheek" and to be forgiving.

While heartbreaking, we can view these times as a learning experience and opportunity to see God's hand at work through trials. Our sons have learned that they did not walk alone but that the Holy Spirit continues to be their companion. Even through the most difficult times we continue to learn to trust in the Lord and not on our own understanding as we are taught in Proverbs 3:5. Had we not had a foundation of faith, rooted in Scripture since the early preschool days, the pitfalls of growing up could lead to rebellious and resentful hearts in our family. While the raising of our children is not yet over, we give thanks be to God that this has not been the case; and we continue to keep a vigilant and watchful eye.

How I would love to see forgiveness seminars and assemblies in our schools. If only the principal had the privilege of praying for the students and guiding them to consider the others better than themselves.

Our children are the children of the community. Our children need to be trained in many things from a young age. If we can teach them to seek first the kingdom of God and to think before they act or speak; by the time they are teenagers their self-control will be more fully in place and the lure of physical violence, sex, drugs and crime will not hold the attraction of immediate gratification for the teen that has been trained from preschool to seek better and wait on the Lord. This is my hope and my prayer.

Chapter 8

Come Together

Do not merely listen to the Word and herby deceive yourselves, do what it says, James 1:22. As a church, as parents and as educators the time to act is now. The focus of this book is the benefit of teaching Christian values in the preschool years. This is in no way suggesting that our ministry and service to teenaged children and young adults is not vital. My urging is that Christian education be embraced in regards to our preschool aged children; that early childhood education would not just be considered babysitting but as intellectual, physical, social, emotional and spiritual equipping. Teaching them of God's core biblical principles is vital, practical and urgent.

I would appear that in these twenty-first century times are we are a nation with youth who are educationally and morally at risk. Drugs, violence and immorality are prevalent in our society and would seem to be targeting the most vulnerable which would be our young people. One would question if anyone is responsible and will be held accountable for the breakdown of our children's behavior. As a preschool teacher I have witnessed on a daily basis our three to four year olds displaying remarkably unkind behavior towards each other. While I am not employed in a Christian school, my Christianity goes with me where I go and so it is that my Christian values and my belief system are in my classroom, they are in me. When I am in the presence of preschool bully tactics, I know in my heart I must intervene. It causes me to pause, reflect on why a young child would exhibit un-Christian behavior and remind myself to view them as Christ does. As God is the potter and we are the clay, so it is my obligation to introduce my young students to the idea of considering others ahead of themselves. To assist in molding them into the moral people they are meant to become. Children are not born knowing how to think about other people's feelings, they need to be taught.

Some children respond well to the idea of treating each other the way they want to be treated. Others will defy this idea and the adult introducing it, having never been trained that the world does not revolve around themselves and the things that they want. They are ambivalent to the fact that other people have feelings. These children need consistent and gentle training. Children from both Christian and non-Christian homes will surely benefit from the character training that can be found in Jesus' Sermon on the Mount. In Matthew chapters 5-7 Jesus taught and set the example for the things we should teach to our children; those who are blessed are the poor in spirit, those that mourn, the meek, those who hunger and thirst after righteousness, the merciful, the pure in heart, the peacemakers, blessed are they which are persecuted for righteousness'' sake. We are to rejoice and teach our children to rejoice for the spirit of the Lord will bless, provide for and preserve.

Children who are being raised in the faith need to be encouraged that their godly character training extends outside the boundaries of the Sunday school class. Preschool aged children have the opportunity to accept character training and incorporate godly traits into their personalities as they develop over time. As a member of the body of Christ it is my obligation and the responsibility of each individual Christian to show kindness, guidance and good will to any and every child. The most troubled and seemingly unlovable child in the neighborhood needs to hear a good word from those of us who call ourselves "Christian" as we remember that we are saved to serve. It is what is known in my Catholic tradition as the New Evangelism; the idea isn't new at all really but is a renewal of that biblical principle to raise up disciples and to be fishers of men, in this case, fishers of children. We need to teach children that morality isn't anything that you decide it to be, as it so often is in our feel good society. Children need to be brought up being taught that morality is outlined in God's word, not for our convenience, but for His perfect will and plan for our lives. The bible is a guide to values that is beneficial not only to the self but all mankind.

We have a parental responsibility to our own children and we have one to the children of the community, not only to the children of the church, for every child belongs to God. We need to begin by guarding our own hearts, setting before our eyes those things that are holy and demonstrate Christian values with prudence and wisdom.

As educators and as a church we are to put on the full armor of God, Ephesians 6:10-18. We must be fully equipped as we begin spiritual preparations. This endeavor of educating our children we are about to embark on is more than supplying our preschoolers with bible stories, songs and videos. We are preparing to go on a journey, a competition which my give every appearance of becoming a battle, to win their young hearts and minds for Christ.

This effort will encompass learning how to spend time with and talk to our children, becoming examples of Christian maturity and adulthood that the children can look up to and rely on. It will require patience and kindness, gentleness and self-control as we begin to raise them in His ways. There will be times when it may seem like a fruitless effort but God's word will not be returned void, it shall accomplish and prosper, Isaiah 55:11.

It has been said that raising children is not for the faint hearted; never has a more true statement been spoken, in my opinion. We will struggle, pray, strive and rejoice to love these children as Christ loves them. Through the anointing of the Holy One we will bring the good news of His redemptive love to children. We will toil to protect them as they grow, shielding them from harmful worldly influences until the time comes when they are emotionally, spiritually and psychologically able to protect themselves; and our work will not be done in vain for God's word will not return void.

We are called as Christians to be in a relationship with Jesus Christ. It is our obligation to bring our preschool aged children into this relationship also. The church, that collective body of believers, needs to learn to value its children and have the patience to spend time with them and mentor them, encourage and direct their paths. Most importantly if we expect our young people to live out their lives with good morals, values and faith then we need to be in the practice of living in the presence of God ourselves first.

For those who feel called to lead or participate in a church youth group there is a need to see the youth as God sees them, through the eyes of Jesus. We, who work in the church youth ministry must move past our anxiety of getting to know the young people, put aside curriculum evaluations and activity planning and just learn to be around and in the company of our youth. Allow me to indicate that spending time with children is a privilege, an honor and must be done in all propriety with the wellbeing of the child in mind.

Books, workshops and software with ministry resources have a place and are useful but cannot substitute for drawing close to the youth of the church, getting to know them, having a heart for their cares and their hopes and just simply spending time with them. I believe that while it would seem to be an obvious requirement in working in preschool and youth ministry, but there are many adults who simply do not know how to accomplish being in the company of young people and are not comfortable in this capacity. Kids can make adults nervous, feel awkward and uncomfortable.

To be with someone is to be present in mind and in attention as to who the young people are, where they are and what they need. To be with someone is to put your own agenda, plans and ideas aside and simply come up alongside each individual and meet them emotionally and spiritually. It happens often in youth ministry that the leaders are busy reading from a guide, following a lesson plan or adhering to a pre-planned activity and are not actively practicing the act of being with their youth. Our young people face many challenges in their lives and need to have a mature adult who will listen to them, share experiences and support them. Being with young people is a conscious act of will to fully immerse oneself into the presence of another, to listen, to care and to respond in love.

I have learned from my experience with youth ministry and early childhood education that it isn't enough to schedule activities and a time to have a youth group meeting; showing up early to set up your area and keeping them occupied while sprinkling scriptures into the time spent together. Being with youth is about being the eyes, heart and hands of Jesus to the youth group, collectively and individually.

Our desire and purpose as a church should be to help our children become alive in Jesus, to nurture their relationships and their Christian daily life. Our efforts will yield a harvest as the children grow and flourish in the knowledge of God. Our calling as a church is to move beyond providing child care but to embrace the children and share the love of the Lord with them. Just as Jesus came alongside his disciples and showed them the only way to God, our goal is to become like Christ and our lives should reflect His love and Holy presence.

Jesus as the Master Teacher has taught us how to teach our children responsibility. For the good of our children, society and future of the church and family we must instill a sense of values, respect and responsibility. To begin we must teach that each individual is responsible for his or her actions, thoughts, choices and responses. This concept was taught in the parables of the talents and the unfaithful servant in Matthew 25:15 and also in Luke 12:47-48. Early training in the preschool years should offer responsibilities to our children methodically and watchfully. We must bear in mind developmentally appropriate practices and assess each child according to the best of their abilities, as instructed in Galatians 4:1. It is only in providing learning opportunities that our children can take the steps to maturity.

Accountability is the key to the foundation of learning responsibility. To train our children in keeping their obligations is as important cognitive and general knowledge skills. When parents and educators do not teach the children of the early education years how to be accountable and answer for their actions they will eventually have rebellious natures to contend with as it is written in 1 Samuel 2:22-26 and 3:13.

Consequences are often the most painful lessons of all but it is written that it is good for a man to bear the yoke in his youth in Lamentations 3:27. Children must learn from an early age that consequences have heavy and serious implications that reach out beyond our own comfort but affect those around us and who interact with us. When we model the behaviors taught in the beatitudes and keep ourselves to the high standard of Christian values we can be encouraged that our children will seek after the potter who molds us into a creation that is after His own image.

Luke 6:40, “Everyone who is fully trained will be like his teacher.” As a Christian educator and as a student my ultimate goal is to become like my teacher who is Jesus Christ. My personal goal is to continually challenge myself to be in study, re-energizing my enthusiasm for God's Word and His purpose. It is only from the overflow of a full life can we successfully teach. If an individual stops growing in their personal and spiritual development, they become stagnant and eventually unable to teach.

As a teacher I am to be primarily a student. I must keep growing and changing as my understanding of God's Word develops. His Word, which does not change, instructs me to grow in the grace and knowledge of our Lord Jesus Christ, asking myself continually through evaluation, "How can I improve?" To be a good teacher and to identify a good teacher one must be faithful, available and teachable. The teacher must be teachable in order to teach others, learning is a process that never ends.

Those who are called to teach are to press onward toward the goal, which God has called us to do; that is to mold to the standard that Jesus has set which requires a commitment to change and to develop. Jesus grew in wisdom, in stature, in favor with God and with men. It is my personal goal to integrate my areas of growth so that the needs of the child in the early educational years can take their first faith steps. Effective teaching is about being an influence on a student so that he or she can develop in the fullness of all that God created them to be.

Proverbs 20:11 tell us that even a child is known by his actions. In all of our training, guiding and nurturing the Gospel of Christ must be central in all that we do. As we, the members of the church go forth to train, edify and equip, let us do so not for the benefit of building congregational programs or for increasing numbers in church membership. Let us train up these children in the way they should go, not for our vanity and pride, but rather let us go forth, living lives of obedience.

Most importantly let us lead these children by example, living lives worthy of their love and admiration. Model Christian values, morals and behavior in the true and loving manner that Jesus did when he walked on Earth. Let us be mindful to teach as he taught his disciples; to love the Lord our God, to love one another, to be merciful, gentle, kind, and forgiving. My prayer is that I have taught my children by example to be charitable, to be giving, to be slow to anger, to be prayerful in all things and to have a daily walk with God. My hope is to be an example to be humble, to seek God's wisdom and to be quick to ask for forgiveness when I fall short of these goals, and I will, we all will. Teach them to be peacemakers. It is often said that there is no guidebook to parenting but I suggest that there is; God's word written in the Holy Bible will show us how to raise them, how to train them. This is not to exasperate them thereby leading them into rebellion but to love and nurture and draw them closer to God, to Jesus, through Him with Him and in Him, in the unity of the Holy Spirit. Teach children of the early childhood years with a loving heart, with the eyes and the Sacred Heart of Jesus and with a Christian worldview for the glory of God and the completion of His work, and raise them in His ways.

References

Essa, E. (2007). *Introduction to early childhood education*. Clifton Park, NY: Thomson Delmar Learning.

Houdmann, S. M. (n.d.). *Why are so many young people falling away from the faith?*Retrieved September 6, 2011, from http://www.gotquestions.org/falling-away.html

Hu, W. (2011, August 20). *Bullying Law Puts New Jersey Schools on Spot - NYTimes.com*. Retrieved January 5, 2012, from http://www.nytimes.com/2011/08/31/nyregion/bullying-law-puts-new-jersey-schools-on-spot.html?pagewanted=all&_r=0

Reed, J., & Prevost, R. (1993). *A History of Christian Education*. Nashville, TN: Broadman and Holman Publishers.

Van Biema, D. (2007, March 22). *The Case for Teaching The Bible - TIME*. Retrieved June 5, 2010, from http://content.time.com/time/magazine/article/0,9171,1601845,00.html

ABOUT THE AUTHOR

Mary Annthipie Bane is a wife and mother of three sons, a former homeschooler and an early childhood educator.

Mary has over fifteen years of Christian service and ministry experience. She holds a Bachelor of Biblical Studies from Ames Christian University and a Master of Christian Education from Andersonville Theological Seminary.

Also by the author
"Following the Shepherd's Staff"

Look for these titles coming soon
"Following the Shepherd's Voice"
"Impulsive"

and the following Christian Fiction titles

"To Have and to Hold"
"A Life to Belong To"
"A Wolf in the Sheepfold"
"The Ornament Box"

Visit the Author Online at

www.facebook.com/maryannthipiebane

and

www.maryannthipiebane.com

5699562R00089

Printed in Great Britain
by Amazon.co.uk, Ltd.,
Marston Gate.